LOOKING FORWARD TO
the nativity

LOOKING FORWARD TO
the nativity

Jon Farrar

Tyndale House Publishers, Inc., Carol Stream, Illinois

Visit Tyndale's exciting Web site at www.tyndale.com

TYNDALE and Tyndale's quill logo are registered trademarks of Tyndale House Publishers, Inc.

Looking Forward to the Nativity

Copyright © 2006 by The Livingstone Corporation. All rights reserved.

Cover photo copyright © by Tom Walker/Getty Images. All rights reserved.

Designed by Jacqueline L. Noe

Previously published in 2000 as *Looking Forward to Christmas* by Baker Books under ISBN 0-8010-1200-7, in association with The Livingstone Corporation.

Looking Forward to the Nativity first published by Tyndale House Publishers, Inc. in 2006.

Scripture quotations are taken from the *Holy Bible*, New Living Translation, copyright © 1996, 2004. Used by permission of Tyndale House Publishers, Inc., Carol Stream, Illinois 60188. All rights reserved.

ISBN-13: 978-1-4143-1502-7
ISBN-10: 1-4143-1502-3

Printed in the United States of America

12 11 10 09 08 07 06
7   6   5   4   3   2   1

contents

introduction

The Christmas season is filled not only with great joy but also with eager anticipation. Children yearn for Christmas morning, with its ribbons and wrappings, stockings and gifts.

Often, the days leading up to Christmas can be harried, with presents to be bought and wrapped and goodies to be baked. Sometimes in the hustle and bustle of the season, the reason we celebrate gets hopelessly lost.

Looking Forward to the Nativity can help your family savor the Christmas season. Beginning with December 1, take some time each day to gather your children around you for reflection and prayer. Read the short story and related Scripture passage that illustrate the excitement, the wonder, and the true meaning of Christmas. Then encourage your children to participate in the simple, yet meaningful, family

activity to further enhance their anticipation
of the celebration of Jesus' birth. *Looking Forward to the Nativity* shows your children how
people throughout human history—from
Adam and Eve to King David to the Virgin
Mary—looked forward to the birth of Jesus in
the same way that your children are looking
forward to this year's Christmas. On December
1, you'll start with the story of Adam and Eve
and why they yearned for the promised Savior.
As you read through December's readings with
your children, you'll realize with them that
many of the important people of the Bible
were looking forward to the Nativity. From
December 17 through December 25, you'll
read a little of the Christmas story every night
to your children.

The Advent Season
As you read daily devotions during the month
of December, you'll be doing what many Christians have done for thousands of years. Christians have been counting the days before
Christmas since the sixth century A.D. In that

century, a church council established the season of Advent—the four weeks before Christmas—and invited Christians to fast and pray during those weeks. Today, many Christians use the four weeks of Advent to remind themselves of the story of Jesus' coming (the word *Advent* means "coming").

You can calculate exactly when Advent begins by finding the Sunday nearest November 30. Depending on what day Christmas is, the Advent season can last anywhere from twenty-two to twenty-eight days. *Looking Forward to the Nativity* starts the devotional readings on December 1 to make it easiest to create a daily habit of reading about Christmas during the busy holiday season.

The Advent Wreath
During the season of Advent, a green Advent wreath with flickering candles has served as a gentle reminder of the true meaning of Christmas for many Christians throughout the centuries. Traditionally, the wreath has consisted of four candles placed in a circle

of evergreen branches. Sometimes a fifth candle—the Christ candle—is placed in the center. The circle represents the unending love of God, and the evergreen branches represent eternal life.

On the first Sunday of Advent, the first candle is lit. Then on each of the three following Sundays, an additional candle is lit. Each candle represents another week of Advent. The glowing flames are reminders of how people throughout the centuries awaited Jesus' birth with great hope and joy. Usually the candles are blue, a color that symbolizes hope in God's promises. Sometimes they are purple, a royal color signifying Jesus' kingship. Finally, on Christmas Day the white Christ candle in the center is lit.

An Advent wreath placed in a central location in your home—on a dining room table or on a fireplace mantle—can be the perfect place for you to gather your children for the short stories in *Looking Forward to the Nativity*. Each of the candles can represent a part of the Christmas story.

FIRST WEEK—the promise candle symbolizes
God's promises to Abraham, Isaac, and other
Israelites. Through their family, all people
would one day be blessed.

SECOND WEEK—the prophet's candle reminds
us of the prophets of Israel who foretold
a coming Savior—a great High Priest,
a Prophet, and a King.

THIRD WEEK—John the Baptist's candle
symbolizes John the Baptist's warning to
the Israelites that Jesus was coming soon.

FOURTH WEEK—Mary's candle reminds us that
Mary believed the angel's announcement
of good news and rejoiced in Jesus' coming.

CHRISTMAS DAY—the Christ candle represents
Jesus, the Light of the World.

Christians have used the candles of the Advent
wreath to symbolize other ideas as well. For
instance, some call the first candle the promise
candle; the second, the Bethlehem candle; the
third, the shepherds' candle; the fourth, the
angels' candle. Whether or not you use an
Advent wreath, use this devotional, *Looking*

Forward to the Nativity, to remind your children of the great number of people who *yearned* for their Savior, who looked forward to the coming of Jesus.

The Seed
of the Christmas Story

It was the beginning of all time, the start of human history. There was a garden called Eden. Within that garden, God planted the seed of the Christmas story.

As Adam and Eve walked around the Garden of Eden, God told them they could eat any of its fruit, except the fruit from the tree of the knowledge of good and evil.

But one day, history was forever changed. Adam and Eve ate some fruit from the tree God had told them not to eat from. The devil, in the form of a serpent, had tempted them to demand their own way. Because Adam and

Eve disobeyed God, he threw them out of the garden.

Although God was angry, he promised that someday a Savior, one of Adam and Eve's own seed, or offspring, would come to overthrow all evil and the devil as represented by the serpent in this story. Adam and Eve looked forward to that day. That day of course is Christmas, the birthday of Jesus—Eve's Seed and our Savior.

Bible Promise

The LORD God said to the serpent, "Because you have done this, you are cursed more than all animals, domestic and wild. You will crawl on your belly, groveling in the dust as long as you live. And I will cause hostility between you and the woman, and between your offspring and her offspring. He will strike your head, and you will strike his heel."
—Genesis 3:14-15

Prayer

Dear Jesus, during this Christmas season we're reminded of the sacrifice you made in coming to earth as a baby. We, like Adam and Eve, know we aren't perfect. We need a Savior. Thank you for coming to save us. Amen.

Family Activity
Sing a verse of "O Come, O Come, Emmanuel" with your children. Throughout the ages, this hymn has been sung during the first week of Advent. Explain to your children that *Emmanuel* is another name for Jesus and means "God with us."

> O come, O come, Emmanuel,
> And ransom captive Israel,
> That mourns in lonely exile here
> Until the Son of God appear.
> Rejoice! Rejoice! Emmanuel
> Shall come to thee, O Israel!

A Brave Journey

Abram (or Abraham, as God named him later)
lived in a land called Ur. One day, God told
him to leave his friends and family and travel
to a faraway land. God promised Abraham
many rewards if he would obey this command.
One reward was that Abraham's family would
grow into a great and mighty nation. The most
important reward though was that through
Abraham's family God would bless all nations.

But there was one problem. Abraham and
his wife Sarai (later named Sarah) had no son,
no one to inherit these wonderful promises. It
seemed impossible that they would ever have a

baby, for both of them were so old. Abraham
had no idea how God's promises could come
true. Yet he believed and bravely set out to
that distant land. He looked forward to the day
when all the world would be blessed through
his family. That day was Christmas, the day
when Jesus—both an offspring of Abraham and
the very Son of God—was born. Through Jesus,
all people would be blessed—a fulfillment of
a promise made long before to a man named
Abraham.

Bible Promise
*"I will make you into a great nation. I will bless you
and make you famous, and you will be a blessing to
others. I will bless those who bless you and curse
those who treat you with contempt. All the families
on earth will be blessed through you."*
—Genesis 12:2-3

Prayer
God, help us to depend on your leading in our
lives. Sometimes we're afraid to try something
new. But you're a God of fresh beginnings, as

you proved in the story of Abraham. Thank you for blessing us through Abraham's family line, through Jesus Christ our Savior. Amen.

Family Activity

Show your children a map or a globe. Ask them how they would feel about going to a faraway land. Would they be excited? Would they be afraid? Ask them what they would do if they could never return home. Would they refuse to go? Point to the places where your relatives live. Show your children places they themselves have visited. Point to faraway places such as China, India, or Africa. If you know some missionaries, show your children where missionaries live. Discuss how Abraham must have felt when he left his home for a distant, unknown land.

The Ultimate Test

Just as God had promised, Sarah gave birth to a baby boy. The young Isaac was truly a miracle child, and he brought much joy to Abraham and Sarah.

Then one day, God told Abraham to take Isaac to a mountain far away. It wasn't a happy journey, for God had asked Abraham to give up Isaac, his only son. Abraham didn't know how he could live without his son—the boy in whom he had placed his hopes. Yet God had spoken, so Abraham obeyed.

When Abraham reached the mountain, an angel of the Lord called out, "Abraham!

Abraham! Don't hurt your son. The Lord knows now that you trust him so much you won't withhold your only son. You have passed God's test. Because of this, your family will grow into a nation through which the Savior will come."

From then on Abraham treasured his son all the more. Isaac was a gift from the Lord. Through Isaac's family would come a Savior— Jesus Christ our Lord.

Bible Promise

"Because you have obeyed me and have not withheld even your son, your only son, I swear by my own name that I will certainly bless you. I will multiply your descendants beyond number, like the stars in the sky and the sand on the seashore. Your descendants will conquer the cities of their enemies. And through your descendants all the nations of the earth will be blessed—all because you have obeyed me."

—Genesis 22:16

Prayer

Lord, like Abraham, you didn't withhold your only Son. Instead, you sent him to earth to save us from our sins. Thank you for your great gift! Help us to be more like you—wholehearted in our giving to you and to others. Amen.

Family Activity

Have your children bring their favorite toy to you. Discuss with them what it means to give away something they love and cherish. Would they give away their favorite toy? their favorite pet? Explain to them that God gave his only Son to save us. Help your children think of one thing they can give back to God as a thank-you for giving them his Son.

Jacob's Restless Night

Bright stars filled the night sky as Jacob sat alone on a rock. This youngest son of Isaac had been traveling all day. He was dusty and tired. He needed to rest, but he didn't have a pillow or a tent. All he could do was roll a small rock closer and use it as a pillow for his sleepy head.

Jacob fell sound asleep and dreamed of a stairway that reached far into heaven. Angels—more than he could count—were going up and down this heavenly staircase. At the top stood God himself! His voice thundered throughout the earth. "I am the God of your grandfather Abraham, and your father, Isaac. I promise that

your family will own this land. Your family will
grow into a nation that will, in turn, bless all
peoples and all nations."

Suddenly, Jacob woke up. "Surely this is the
house of the living God," he said to himself.
"God has given me a place in his great plan."
So Jacob, like his grandfather Abraham, and
his father, Isaac, before him, believed God's
promise. Through their family, God would bless
all nations.

Bible Promise

*At the top of the stairway stood the LORD, and he
said, "I am the LORD, the God of your grandfather
Abraham, and the God of your father, Isaac. The
ground you are lying on belongs to you. I am giving
it to you and your descendants. Your descendants
will be as numerous as the dust of the earth! They
will spread out in all directions—to the west and the
east, to the north and the south. And all the families
of the earth will be blessed through you and your
descendants. What's more, I am with you, and I
will protect you wherever you go."*

—Genesis 28:13-15

Prayer

Father God, thank you for keeping the promises you made to Abraham, Isaac, and Jacob. Thank you for sending your Son, Jesus, to save and bless us. Help us to be as loyal to you as you are to your promises. Amen.

Family Activity

If you live in an area where snow has fallen, consider bundling up and going outside to make "snow angels." (Have your children lie on their backs in the snow and move their arms to make "wings.") If you prefer to stay inside, draw outlines of angels on white construction paper and have your children cut them out. Cut out a ladder as well. Discuss with your children how the angels reminded Jacob of God's promises.

A Passover Lamb

After many years, the number of Abraham's children and grandchildren increased. They were called Hebrews, and they lived in Egypt, where Egypt's evil king had made them slaves. Their life was very difficult, so they cried out to the Lord their God.

God heard their cries and sent Moses to order the Egyptians to let the Hebrews go. But the king refused to let them go. Instead, he made them work even harder.

Finally, God had enough of this stubborn king. He would free his people, even if it meant taking away every one of Egypt's firstborn sons.

God wanted the Hebrews to always remember his power and might, so he commanded Moses and Aaron to tell them to sacrifice a Passover lamb that very night. The Hebrews were to paint the lamb's blood on the doorposts of their homes. This would save their own first-born sons, and it would represent God's love for them. It would also point to Jesus—God's only Son—who would one day show his Father's love to everyone.

Bible Promise

Christ, our Passover Lamb, has been sacrificed for us. So let us celebrate the festival, not with the old bread of wickedness and evil, but with the new bread of sincerity and truth.

—1 Corinthians 5:7-8

Prayer

READER: Dear Jesus, reading about the Passover reminds us of your purpose in coming to this earth. You are our Passover Lamb. You gave up your own life for our sins.

CHILDREN: Thank you, Jesus, our Passover Lamb.

READER: In this season of joyful giving, may we not forget how much you gave up for us.

CHILDREN: Thank you, Jesus, our Passover Lamb.

ALL: Amen.

Family Activity
Place a lamb ornament on your tree to represent the Passover Lamb and to remind you of Jesus, the person who saved you through his own death on the cross. If you don't have a lamb ornament, you can make one out of construction paper. Use cotton balls to add "wool" to your lamb.

A Mountain Set on Fire

The Hebrews—freed from their Egyptian task-masters—gathered at the foot of Mount Sinai. There, God would give them his law. With loud thunder and lightning, God did speak, and Mount Sinai was set on fire.

The people shook in fear. "Don't let God speak. His voice frightens us," they pleaded. "Have someone go between us and him, for he is so great and we are so frail."

The Lord God agreed. For now, Moses would be God's spokesman and prophet. Yet God also promised the Israelites that one day he would send a greater prophet. The Hebrews held on to this promise, waiting for this great prophet. Jesus is this great Prophet and Teacher. His words are to be followed; his life is our model. This is why we enjoy Christmas Day—Jesus' birthday.

Bible Promise

God was fulfilling what all the prophets had foretold about the Messiah—that he must suffer these things. Moses said, "The LORD your God will raise up for you a Prophet like me from among your own people. Listen carefully to everything he tells you." Then Moses said, "Anyone who will not listen to that Prophet will be completely cut off from God's people." Starting with Samuel, every prophet spoke about what is happening today.

—Acts 3:18, 22-24

Prayer

Lord, in this busy season, we often don't take the time to be silent and wait for you to speak. But we know that you still want us to listen to the preachers and teachers of your Word. Thank you for sending Jesus, the ultimate Prophet and Teacher. Amen.

Family Activity

Christmas is the time of year when we should remember to say thank you to the people who have meant a lot to us. Suggest that your children think of a way to say thanks to their teachers this week. Although Jesus is our ultimate teacher and deserves our wholehearted thanks, we can learn to be grateful by thanking those who teach us every day.

Aaron and God's Holy Tent

Moses had a brother named Aaron. From the start, Aaron, with his long shepherd's rod, had been with Moses; together they had confronted the evil king, Pharaoh.

At Mount Sinai, God told Aaron to be a priest. Aaron—dressed in special robes—was to represent the people before the Lord in God's Holy Tent, the Tabernacle. There, Aaron would pray for the people and ask God's forgiveness for his sin and theirs. But before entering God's Holy Tent, Aaron had to sacrifice animals as symbols of the seriousness of the people's sin.

Later, God promised the Israelites that he

would provide a perfect high priest. This priest would be better than Aaron, and he wouldn't have to sacrifice animals. He would stand on his own right before God forever. This high priest is Jesus, whose birthday we celebrate.

Bible Promise

Christ did not honor himself by assuming he could become High Priest. No, he was chosen by God, who said to him, "You are my Son. Today I have become your Father." And in another passage God said to him, "You are a priest forever in the order of Melchizedek." While Jesus was here on earth, he offered prayers and pleadings, with a loud cry and tears, to the one who could rescue him from death. And God heard his prayers because of his deep reverence for God.
—Hebrews 5:5-7

Prayer

Lord God, you are holy. We cannot come to you on our own. Only Jesus, our perfect high priest, can cleanse us from our sin. Forgive our sins and take them away. Help us to live holy

lives. May your name be honored in all that
we do. Amen.

Family Activity

Help your children understand what the word
holy means. Show them two pieces of white
paper—one blank and one with some kind of
stain on it. The blank paper represents God's
holiness. He is perfect; the stain of sin cannot
touch him. On the other hand, the stained
paper represents our sinful lives. When we
believe in Jesus, he washes our sin away, and our
lives become like a clean piece of paper. Then,
sing a song about God's holiness, for example,
"Holy, Holy, Holy."

A Surprising Harvest

Long ago, two widows lived together in Bethlehem. The older woman was named Naomi, and the younger was her daughter-in-law, Ruth. The two were very poor.

In that same town lived a rich man named Boaz. His fields were overflowing with barley, so one day Ruth went to gather whatever was left after the great harvest. To her surprise, there was plenty to gather.

"Where did you get all this grain?" Naomi asked when Ruth got home that day.

"From a man named Boaz," Ruth replied. "He saw to it that I got all this grain."

"Boaz is a rich relative of ours!" Naomi exclaimed. "He can be our family's redeemer: He can protect us, provide for us, and save us from poverty!"

Boaz made Ruth his wife, and Naomi became a part of his family. The people of Bethlehem rejoiced. Though no one knew it that day, the story of Boaz's great love pointed to a coming redeemer—another, greater Savior. Hundreds of years later, Jesus—a distant relative of Boaz—was born in Bethlehem on Christmas Day. Jesus, out of his great love for us, has offered to save all who turn to him.

Bible Promise

Ruth gathered barley there all day, and when she beat out the grain that evening, it filled an entire basket. She carried it back into town and showed it to her mother-in-law. Ruth also gave her the roasted grain that was left over from her meal.

"Where did you gather all this grain today?" Naomi asked. "Where did you work? May the Lord *bless the one who helped you!"*

So Ruth told her mother-in-law about the man in

*whose field she had worked. She said, "The man
I worked with today is named Boaz."*

*"May the LORD bless him!" Naomi told her
daughter-in-law. "He is showing his kindness to
us as well as to your dead husband. That man
is one of our closest relatives, one of our family
redeemers."*

—Ruth 2:17-20

Prayer
Jesus, our Redeemer, you fill us with joy. You
give us so much. Open our eyes, Lord, to those
around us who don't have as much as we have.
Help us, Lord, to be a blessing to them as Boaz
was a blessing to Ruth and Naomi. Amen.

Family Activity
Put grain in your bird feeder, or feed some
squirrels or geese with your children. As you
feed these animals, talk about God's generous
provision for your family. Help your children
name a few things that God has provided for
them. Consider taking them to a soup kitchen
to help the less fortunate in your community.

The Sons of Eli

There once was a good priest named Eli. But his sons were very evil; they bullied the people and even stole from them.

One day an old, wise prophet came to Eli with strong words of warning. "Why do you allow this to happen?" the prophet asked. "You let your sons steal from God. They steal the animals and the food that has been given to the Lord your God. Therefore the Lord will not let your family serve as priests forever. He will appoint a faithful priest who will serve him forever."

Faithful Israelites welcomed the prophet's

message. They couldn't wait for the day when a good priest would come, one who would pray for them. Jesus is this faithful priest. He is in heaven today, pleading for you and me before God our Father. The Hebrews of Eli's day looked forward to Jesus' birthday. We look to Christmas Day to celebrate the birthday of our high priest in heaven.

Bible Promise
"I will raise up a faithful priest who will serve me and do what I desire. I will establish his family, and they will be priests to my anointed kings forever."
—1 Samuel 2:35

Prayer
Jesus, you know how much it hurts when we see the bad examples some grown-ups set. Thank you for being our perfect high priest, the one who doesn't seek to have his own needs met before anyone else's. Your tender care gives us true hope and great joy. Amen.

Family Activity

If you haven't already done so, make a prayer list for the Christmas season. On poster board or a sheet of paper, write the concerns your children want to pray for as a family, or list each need on a slip of paper and put the slips in a jar. Have each family member draw out one prayer request every day. Keep track of the times when you receive answers to your prayers.

King David and His Palace

One day, King David sat on his royal throne and looked over everything he owned: a large palace made of sturdy cedars and a vast kingdom headed by twelve tribal leaders.

"How can I live in this fine palace," he sighed to Nathan, his friend, "while the ark of God stays in a flimsy tent?"

Nathan, a prophet and wise leader, replied, "God has spoken. He doesn't need a palace or a home of any kind. He already lives high above the tallest cedar and near all his devoted believers. And God doesn't need your gifts," Nathan explained. "He placed you on your throne. God

promises to you this day that he will place
your son on that same throne to reign forever
and ever."

From then on, David longed to see the day
when his perfect son would reign forever. That
Son of David is Jesus, and the day David longed
for is Christmas—the birthday of the King of
kings.

Bible Promise

*"The LORD declares that he will make a house for
you—a dynasty of kings! For when you die and are
buried with your ancestors, I will raise up one of
your descendants, your own offspring, and I will
make his kingdom strong. He is the one who will
build a house—a temple—for my name. And I will
secure his royal throne forever. I will be his father,
and he will be my son."*

—2 Samuel 7:11-14

Prayer

Jesus, Son of David, you are the King of kings
and Lord of lords. In this day of constant
change, it is comforting to know that you're

always the same. Your kingdom will never pass
away. For that, we're grateful. Amen.

Family Activity
Buy some premade cookie dough—the kind
you can decorate yourself. Let the children
decorate the cookies with crowns as symbols
of the coming King of kings. While the cookies
are baking, make some hot chocolate and look
at photo albums. Share with your children how
you looked forward to their coming before
they were born. Unlike David, you didn't have
to wait hundreds of years before your children
arrived!

In Need
of a Friend

Long ago, a rich and honest man named Job
lived in the land of Uz. He owned thousands of
sheep and camels and a great number of oxen
and donkeys.

One day, Job's life was turned upside down.
His oxen, camels, and donkeys were stolen, and
his sheep and servants died in a fire. Worst of all,
his oldest son's house caved in, killing all Job's
sons and daughters, who were visiting there. Job
was brokenhearted.

"Why has this happened?" Job moaned.
"What have I done to deserve such great harm?"
Job's wife, friends, and neighbors didn't console

him. And so Job sat down in a heap of ashes,
truly alone.

Yet Job still looked to God to save him.
"No one will defend me here on earth," he
cried. "But I know my Supporter—my Savior—
is in heaven. He pleads with God on my behalf
as a man would plead for his friend."

Job's hope wasn't misplaced; God did save
him. God restored his good fortune by giving
him more than he had before. Today we know
who our Friend in heaven is—the person to
whom Job looked long ago. On Christmas Day
we celebrate the birth of Jesus, our Friend and
Savior.

Bible Promise

Even now my witness is in heaven.
   My advocate is there on high.
My friends scorn me,
   but I pour out my tears to God.
I need someone to mediate between God and me,
   as a person mediates between friends.
—Job 16:19-21

Prayer

Dear Jesus, thanks for being our Friend and Savior. In those difficult times when our friends here on earth seem to abandon us, it is a comfort to know we can depend on you. You are in heaven, taking up our cause before God Almighty. Help us to show that same compassion and love to our neighbors. Amen.

Family Activity

Ask your children if they know someone who is experiencing a difficult time and needs a friend as Job did. Then discuss with your children how your family can show Christ's love to that person (for example, doing an errand, preparing a meal, or baking some cookies). If your children can't think of anyone in need, help them think of something they can do for the poor in your community.

The Promise of a Son

"The Lord is going to give you a sign: A virgin will give birth to a baby boy, and his name will be Immanuel," the prophet Isaiah proclaimed. "That name means 'God with us.'"

King Ahaz listened carefully to Isaiah. His nation was in trouble, and his neighbors were threatening him, so Ahaz was very worried.

Isaiah had come to Ahaz with a comforting message. God was with him. A son would be born as a sign that God was with his people, the Israelites.

"A child, a son, will be born to us. He will rule as a king, and he will be called Wonderful

Counselor, Mighty God, Everlasting Father, and Prince of Peace!" Isaiah shouted. The Israelites believed this promise and looked forward to the birthday of their King who would be above all kings. On Christmas Day, Isaiah's words of comfort came true. Jesus, our King, was born to the Virgin Mary.

Bible Promise
For a child is born to us,
a son is given to us.
The government will rest on his shoulders.
And he will be called:
Wonderful Counselor, Mighty God,
Everlasting Father, Prince of Peace.
His government and its peace
will never end.
—Isaiah 9:6-7

Prayer
READER: Jesus, we can come to you for help with our problems.

CHILDREN: We thank you, Wonderful Counselor!

READER: You possess all power.

CHILDREN: We praise you, Mighty God!

READER: You provide all that we need.

CHILDREN: We thank you, Everlasting Father.

READER: You protect us so we can lie down in peace.

CHILDREN: We honor you, Prince of Peace. Amen.

Family Activity

Use a poster board or a large piece of construction paper to make a sign bearing the names of Jesus mentioned in the reading above. Older children can write the names for Jesus themselves; younger children can join in the fun of coloring and decorating. Post the sign in a window or on the refrigerator.

The Little Town
of Bethlehem

"Bethlehem, even though you are a small town, one who will rule over Israel will come from you," the prophet Micah announced.

The promise of a coming ruler was the only ray of hope that Micah could give the people of Israel. The people no longer looked to God to protect them. As a result, the Lord was going to allow the country to experience war and destruction.

Yet the people of Israel would not be completely abandoned. In the small town of Bethlehem, a great leader would be born. What a promise! Israel would one day have a mighty ruler. That ruler promised long ago is the baby Jesus. Tucked into the hills of Judea, the small town of Bethlehem became the birthplace of the King of kings.

Bible Promise

But you, O Bethlehem Ephrathah, are only a small village among all the people of Judah. Yet a ruler of Israel will come from you, one whose origins are from the distant past.
—Micah 5:2

Prayer

O Jesus, we don't know why you chose to be born in Bethlehem, that small, overlooked town. You are the King of kings, yet you chose to live in a frail human body. Thank you for coming to this earth to provide salvation for us all. Prepare our hearts for your coming this Christmas season. Amen.

Family Activity

Sing "O Little Town of Bethlehem" with your children.

> O little town of Bethlehem, how still
>   we see thee lie!
> Above thy deep and dreamless sleep
>   the silent stars go by.
> Yet in thy dark streets shineth the
>   everlasting Light;
> The hopes and fears of all the years are
>   met in thee tonight.

A King Is Coming!

Long ago, there lived the great prophet Jeremiah. It was a cruel and godless time to live. In those days, the people were doing whatever they wanted to do. The powerful would lie, cheat, and steal, while the powerless had little or no hope. Their rulers would simply look the other way.

"There will be a time," the prophet Jeremiah declared, "when God is going to place a righteous Branch on the throne of King David. He will do what is right in our land."

What a promise! The helpless would have hope, because a king who did only what was right would one day rule the entire land.

The people listened carefully. They would be able to live in safety! Jeremiah spoke of a king who would be powerful and mighty—a king who would reign forever as their great protector. This mighty King is none other than Jesus. Christmas is his birthday. He is the reason we have a grand celebration.

Bible Promise

"For the time is coming,"
    says the LORD,
"when I will raise up a righteous descendant
    from King David's line.
He will be a King who rules with wisdom.
    He will do what is just and right throughout
        the land.
And this will be his name:
    'The LORD *Is Our Righteousness.'"*
—Jeremiah 23:5-6

Prayer

READER: Dear Jesus, you are the righteous Branch, the one Jeremiah foretold. Today we praise your name and look forward to celebrating your coming to earth.

CHILDREN: Make a joyful noise to the Lord. Hallelujah! Hallelujah!

ALL: Come quickly, Lord Jesus. Amen.

Family Activity

Have the children make small crowns out of construction paper to hang on your Christmas tree. Use some evergreen branches to decorate your home, and mention that Jesus was the righteous Branch Jeremiah prophesied about.

Daniel's Vision

Young Daniel was miles and miles away from his home—the rolling hills of Jerusalem. The king of Babylon had taken over Jerusalem and brought Daniel and his friends to work in his palace.

Far away from his friends and relatives, Daniel relied on God. He knelt to pray three times a day to the Lord, his God. Not even the King's law could stop him. For this, Daniel was thrown into a deep lions' pit. But the hungry, roaring lions that surrounded Daniel couldn't harm him one bit. God was Daniel's protector, and he rescued Daniel from the lions' pit.

Daniel spent the rest of his days in the city of Babylon. In a marvelous vision, God gave Daniel a glimpse into the future. One great day, the Jews would return to the empty streets of Jerusalem. In the distant future, a great heavenly king would reign over the world.

Daniel would never see Jerusalem again, but God's promise was enough. A king from heaven would come to rule all nations. This King's name is Jesus. We, like Daniel, wait for the day when Jesus will return to reign over all nations forever and ever.

Bible Promise

I saw someone like a son of man coming with the clouds of heaven. He approached the Ancient One and was led into his presence. He was given authority, honor, and sovereignty over all the nations of the world, so that people of every race and nation and language would obey him. His rule is eternal—it will never end. His kingdom will never be destroyed.

—Daniel 7:13-14

Prayer

Jesus, you are the strong Lion of Judah, whose coming Daniel saw in a vision. You are the mighty King who will rule all nations. As Daniel did so long ago, we also depend on your protection in the difficult situations we face. Help us to have the courage to face [name a difficult situation your family is facing]. We believe you will deliver us. Amen.

Family Activity

Share times when you depended on God for strength and courage. Let everyone have a turn at telling a story. Sit in a circle and give a ball to whomever will speak first. When that person is done, he or she should toss the ball to the next person. If you have very young children, show them a book filled with pictures of different kinds of animals. Explain how some are big and scary. Then tell them that God is bigger than the largest animal they have ever seen. He helps us when we're scared.

Out of a City's Ruins

Finally the day had come! The Jews were return-
ing to their beloved home, Jerusalem. No longer
would they have to stay in the strange city of
Babylon.

Yet Jerusalem didn't look the same as when
their mothers and fathers had left several years
before. Its tall walls had fallen, and weeds and
thorns had taken the place of gardens.

The Jews had hard work ahead of them.
They had to rebuild the city walls and the temple. When they finally laid the last stone, there
was a grand celebration. The people sang and
rejoiced.

Then the prophet Haggai shouted out at the top of his voice: "A time is coming in the future when the rebuilt temple in Jerusalem will be visited by a great Savior! All the people of the world will tremble before this great King of kings!"

Today we can join in spirit with the Jews who gathered that day to worship and rejoice. God's promises have surely come true. King Jesus, born on Christmas Day, did visit the city of Jerusalem.

Bible Promise

"This is what the LORD of Heaven's Armies says: In just a little while I will again shake the heavens and the earth, the oceans and the dry land. I will shake all the nations, and the treasures of all the nations will be brought to this Temple. I will fill this place with glory, says the LORD of Heaven's Armies. The silver is mine, and the gold is mine, says the LORD of Heaven's Armies. The future glory of this Temple will be greater than its past glory, says the LORD of Heaven's Armies. And

*in this place I will bring peace. I, the LORD
of Heaven's Armies, have spoken!"*
—Haggai 2:6-9

Prayer
Dear Jesus, like Haggai, we celebrate your coming. Rebuild the torn-down places in our lives—
the places where doubt and fear exist instead of
faith and courage. Thank you for always keeping
your word. Help us to place our trust completely
in you and your promises. Amen.

Family Activity
Go caroling as a family. Decide beforehand
which songs you will sing to share the joy
of the Savior's coming with your neighbors.
Or deliver a card or some baked goods to a
neighbor, if caroling isn't your family's favorite
activity.

An Angel's Visit

The Christmas story begins with the priest
Zechariah. He had been praying and praying
for a child but only ended up waiting. His wife
remained childless, and he grew hopeless.

But then one day, he was chosen to offer
prayers and incense in the Temple before God's
sight. What a privilege! While the people stood
outside praying, Zechariah stood inside with
his hands trembling. As the smoke from the
incense spiraled upward, he called out to God
the Almighty.

Suddenly an angel appeared. "Don't be
afraid," he said. "God has heard your prayer.

Your wife, Elizabeth, will give birth to a son. He will be great in God's sight, and he will go before the Lord to make the people ready."

Zechariah was stunned. "A son? A son? How can it be? My wife and I are very old."

"How dare you question the Almighty!" the angel replied. "I am Gabriel, an angel sent from God. Yes, you will have a son just as I say. But because you didn't believe me, you won't speak a word until that joyous day."

Bible Promise

While Zechariah was in the sanctuary, an angel of the Lord appeared to him, standing to the right of the incense altar. Zechariah was shaken and overwhelmed with fear when he saw him. But the angel said, "Don't be afraid, Zechariah! God has heard your prayer. Your wife, Elizabeth, will give you a son, and you are to name him John. You will have great joy and gladness, and many will rejoice at his birth, for he will be great in the eyes of the Lord. He must never touch wine or other alcoholic drinks. He will be filled with the Holy Spirit, even before his birth. And he will turn many Israelites

*to the Lord their God. He will be a man with the
spirit and power of Elijah. He will prepare the
people for the coming of the Lord. He will turn the
hearts of the fathers to their children, and he will
cause those who are rebellious to accept the wisdom
of the godly."*
—Luke 1:11-17

Prayer
Lord, sometimes we're tempted to react in
unbelief as Zechariah did, especially when
we hear news that seems too good to be true.
Help us to remember that with you, nothing is
impossible. With you, we can know the truth.
Amen.

Family Activity
Light a fragrant candle, or prepare mulled cider.
Let the fragrance remind your children of the
incense Zechariah used during his priestly duties
in the Temple. Talk about how Zechariah's son,
John the Baptist, would later prepare the way
for Jesus.

Gabriel's Message for Mary

One day, a bright angel appeared to a young woman named Mary. "Greetings, God has chosen you for a special task," he declared.

Mary, white with fright, couldn't say a thing. *What could this man mean?* she thought.

"You are going to give birth to a son," the archangel Gabriel explained. "And you are to name him Jesus. He will be great, and he will be the Son of the Most High."

How could this be? A son? A baby? "Sir, I'm a virgin," Mary humbly protested.

"The Holy Spirit will cause this to happen,

and the baby will be called the Son of God," the angel cheerfully proclaimed.

"I don't know how this can be. But I am God's servant—his trusted employee. I will do what he wants," Mary agreed. "I will hold and love this special baby."

Bible Promise

God sent the angel Gabriel to Nazareth, a village in Galilee, to a virgin named Mary. She was engaged to be married to a man named Joseph, a descendant of King David. Gabriel appeared to her and said, "Greetings, favored woman! The Lord is with you!" Confused and disturbed, Mary tried to think what the angel could mean. "Don't be afraid, Mary," the angel told her, "for you have found favor with God! You will conceive and give birth to a son, and you will name him Jesus. He will be very great and will be called the Son of the Most High. The Lord God will give him the throne of his ancestor David. And he will reign over Israel forever; his Kingdom will never end!"

—*Luke 1:26-33*

Prayer

Father God, we want to respond to you as Mary did—with hearts open to receive the precious gift of your Son. Lord, help us to view Jesus' birth with fresh eyes this season. Help us never to take for granted that he came to save each one of us. Amen.

Family Activity

Cut out an angel from white construction paper and place it on your Christmas tree. It will stand for the angel's promise to Mary of a baby boy. Take a walk through your neighborhood and look at all the Christmas lights. Remind your children that Jesus is the Light of the World.

Mary's Song

Both Mary and her cousin Elizabeth were going to have a child; one woman was young, the other old. After an angel told Mary about God's marvelous plan, she hurried to see Elizabeth.

When Mary arrived, Elizabeth felt the baby move inside her. Then, at the sound of Mary's voice, the child in Elizabeth's womb leapt for joy.

"Praise God!" Elizabeth said to Mary. "You believed the Lord, and he will surely keep his word."

"Yes, praise God!" Mary proclaimed. Then she sang this song:

"Oh, how my soul praises the Lord. How my

spirit rejoices in God my Savior! For he took notice of his lowly servant girl, and from now on all generations will call me blessed.

"For the Mighty One is holy, and he has done great things for me."

Bible Promise

"Oh, how my soul praises the Lord.
How my spirit rejoices in God my Savior!
For he took notice of his lowly servant girl,
and from now on all generations will call
me blessed.
For the Mighty One is holy,
and he has done great things for me."
—Luke 1:46-49

Prayer

O Lord God, we join Mary in praising you; our souls praise your name, and our spirits rejoice in you. Thank you for your willingness to become one of us, to live and die for our sake. Amen.

Family Activity

Sing "Joy to the World!" with your children.

> Joy to the world! the Lord is come;
> Let earth receive her King;
> Let ev'ry heart prepare Him room,
> And heav'n and nature sing,
> And heav'n and nature sing,
> And heav'n, and heav'n and nature sing.

John the Baptist's Birth

When the time came for Elizabeth to have her baby, she gave birth to a boy. All the neighbors and relatives who gathered rejoiced; they wondered what they should name him. "Zechariah," the father's name, was the most common suggestion.

"No," Elizabeth protested. "John is his name."

"What?" the people exclaimed. "No one in your family has that same name."

They couldn't believe it. John just couldn't be his name.

Finally, they asked the boy's father for a

definite answer. Since Zechariah was still unable to talk, he picked up his tablet and wrote, "His name is John."

The neighbors were surprised at his answer. Then, something even more surprising happened. Suddenly Zechariah could speak, and he began praising God. "Praise the God of Israel, because he has kept the promises he made to his people!" he exclaimed. "And you, my little son," he said, looking down at John, "will be a prophet of the Most High, because you are going to prepare the people for the Lord's coming."

Bible Promise

His father, Zechariah, was filled with the Holy Spirit and gave this prophecy:

"Praise the Lord, the God of Israel,
    because he has visited and redeemed his people.
He has sent us a mighty Savior
    from the royal line of his servant David,
just as he promised
    through his holy prophets long ago.

And you, my little son,
>   *will be called the prophet of the Most High,*
>   *because you will prepare the way for the Lord."*
—*Luke 1:67-70, 76*

Prayer
Lord Jesus, there are so many names that
describe you: Prince of Peace, Mighty God,
Wonderful Counselor. We also call you our
Friend and our Savior. As you called John to be
a prophet who prepared the way for your coming, we too are called to prepare our hearts for
your coming. Amen.

Family Activity
Gather in a circle and take turns listing all the
various names for God; for example, Lamb of
God, Lion of Judah. The first person to duplicate a name is out for that round. Then, play
it again, naming all the Bible people you can
think of. Again, the first person to duplicate a
name is out for that round. Play as many rounds
as time allows. Share with your children the
importance of names. If you have a book that

contains the meaning of names, you might
mention the meaning of some of the names
you've discussed.

Joseph and Mary

Joseph was a hardworking carpenter who was engaged to be married to a young woman named Mary.

One day, Joseph received some startling news: Mary was going to have a baby! *How can this be?* Joseph kept asking himself. *How could my dear Mary betray me?* Bewildered and confused, Joseph lay down and went to sleep.

Then, an angel suddenly appeared. "Don't be afraid," the angel said. "Go ahead and marry your young bride, Mary. The baby she is carrying is Israel's Lord and Savior. And you are to name the baby Jesus, because he is going to save his people from their sins."

Joseph did what the angel said, and he and Mary became husband and wife.

Bible Promise

An angel of the Lord appeared to him in a dream. "Joseph, son of David," the angel said, "do not be afraid to take Mary as your wife. For the child within her was conceived by the Holy Spirit. And she will have a son, and you are to name him Jesus, for he will save his people from their sins." All of this occurred to fulfill the Lord's message through his prophet: "Look! The virgin will conceive a child! She will give birth to a son, and they will call him Immanuel, which means 'God is with us.'"
—Matthew 1:20-23

Prayer

Father of Jesus, thank you for the grace you showed both Mary and Joseph. Thank you for letting your Son grow up in a carpenter's family. May we learn from this example of humility. Amen.

Family Activity

Let your children help you set up a crèche or
Nativity scene if you have one. As the children
place Joseph on the scene, let them review the
story you just read. If you don't have a Nativity
scene, use this opportunity to share a story
from your own courting days. Talk about how
important it is to have a loving home and how
important it was for Mary and Joseph to stay
together.

Simeon and Anna's Long Wait

In the city of Jerusalem lived a good man named Simeon. He believed God's promise that Israel would have a great Savior. The Lord had told Simeon he would see this great deliverer with his own eyes. Simeon held on to God's promises tightly and simply waited. He greeted every day thinking, *Will I meet the Lord of all nations today?*

In that same city—within the Temple courts—a devout woman also waited. Her name was Anna. And night and day, she prayed to her Creator, expecting her Lord and Savior. Although she and Simeon didn't know Joseph and Mary or their baby, they knew their Maker.

They knew God kept his promises, so they waited confidently.

Bible Promise
There was a man in Jerusalem named Simeon. He was righteous and devout and was eagerly waiting for the Messiah to come and rescue Israel. The Holy Spirit was upon him and had revealed to him that he would not die until he had seen the Lord's Messiah.
—Luke 2:25-26

Prayer
Lord, in this day of instant communication, we find waiting very difficult. Yet Simeon and Anna waited many years to see the fulfillment of your promise to send your Son. We too look forward with eagerness to Christmas Day—the day we celebrate Jesus' birth. May our celebration on that joyous day honor you. Amen.

Family Activity
Role-play the story with your children. Have them wear bathrobes, and let them take turns being Simeon and Anna. Explain what the

Temple and its courts looked like. Suggest
that they express with words and gestures how
Simeon and Anna might have felt waiting for
the birth of the Savior.

The Wise Men's Journey

After Jesus was born, a group of wise men set out on a journey. They loaded their camels with gifts of gold, frankincense, and myrrh, for they were searching for a newborn king—the King of the Jews. They had watched his brilliant star rise in the east and followed it to the city of Jerusalem.

"Where is the newborn King of the Jews?" they asked everyone they knew.

King Herod was upset when he heard about the wise men's search. After all, *he* was the king of the Jews, and there would be no other. He called in the priests and the teachers.

"Who is this king? Where was he born?" he asked them.

All the priests and teachers answered, "The prophets have said that in Bethlehem—in that small town of David—the Savior of the Jews would be born."

"Go to Bethlehem and find this King of the Jews," Herod said to the wise men, pretending that he wanted to worship the baby too. With this, the wise men continued their search for Jesus, the great King of the Jews.

Bible Promise

Some wise men from eastern lands arrived in Jerusalem, asking, "Where is the newborn king of the Jews? We saw his star as it rose, and we have come to worship him."

King Herod was deeply disturbed when he heard this, as was everyone in Jerusalem. He called a meeting of the leading priests and teachers of religious law and asked, "Where is the Messiah supposed to be born?"

"In Bethlehem in Judea," they said, "for this is what the prophet wrote:

'And you, O Bethlehem in the land of Judah,
   are not least among the ruling cities
         of Judah,
for a ruler will come from you
   who will be the shepherd for my people
         Israel.'"
—Matthew 2:1-6

Prayer
Dear Lord Jesus, we thank you that we don't
have to search the entire world to find you, as
the wise men did. We can pray to you anywhere
and anytime. May we never stop seeking you
and your will for us, in both good times and bad.
Prepare our hearts during this Christmas season
to worship you. Amen.

Family Activity
Hide an object that represents the baby Jesus
(a cross cut out of construction paper or a manger from a crèche). Let your children pretend
to be wise men looking for Jesus; have them
wear sheets to represent royal robes, and hang
a star from a doorway. After your children have

found the object, compare their excitement in finding the object to the excitement the wise men experienced when they found Jesus.

The Shepherds at Night

The night sky was clear, and stars shone brightly on the shepherds far below. They were watching over their flocks, keeping them safely within sight, so no harm would come to them.

Then all of a sudden, an angel appeared. The shepherds were frightened. "Don't be afraid; I'm bringing good news," the angel said. "Today a Savior has been born in the city of David; he is Christ the Lord." The night sky lit up. Angels appeared all around, singing, "Glory to God and peace on earth!"

As the angels were leaving, the stunned shepherds continued to stare into the sky. Finally

they said to each other: "Let's go to Bethlehem
to see what God has done. Let's find this boy—
our Savior."

Bible Promise

That night there were shepherds staying in the fields
nearby, guarding their flocks of sheep. Suddenly, an
angel of the Lord appeared among them, and the
radiance of the Lord's glory surrounded them. They
were terrified, but the angel reassured them. "Don't
be afraid!" he said. "I bring you good news that will
bring great joy to all people. The Savior—yes, the
Messiah, the Lord—has been born today in
Bethlehem, the city of David! And you will recognize
him by this sign: You will find a baby wrapped snugly
in strips of cloth, lying in a manger."

Suddenly, the angel was joined by a vast host of
others—the armies of heaven—praising God and
saying,

"Glory to God in highest heaven,
    and peace on earth to those with whom God
        is pleased."
—Luke 2:8-14

Prayer

O Lord, our voices join the angels in enthusiastic praise. Jesus, our Savior, has come. May all people acknowledge his glorious name, for with his birth in Bethlehem, the world will never be the same. Christ has come to free us from the chains of sin. To God be the glory forever and ever. Amen.

Family Activity

Discuss with your children what an angel is— a messenger of God. Then gather with your children to sing "Hark! The Herald Angels Sing."

> Hark! The herald angels sing, "Glory
>   to the newborn King;
> Peace on earth, and mercy mild, God
>   and sinners reconciled!"
> Joyful, all ye nations, rise; join the
>   triumph of the skies;
> With th' angelic host proclaim, "Christ
>   is born in Bethlehem!"
> Hark! The herald angels sing, "Glory
>   to the newborn King!"

Jesus' Birthday

Joseph and Mary had traveled a long, long way. As dusk approached, they came to the little town of Bethlehem. Its household lights were a welcome sight, for they were tired.

But Joseph and Mary couldn't find any room at the inn. Bethlehem was packed with people, because Emperor Augustus had called for a census. Each person was required to go to his or her hometown to be counted in this great census.

So with no room at the inn, all Joseph and Mary could find was a modest stable—a place made for donkeys, sheep, and cattle.

That night, the time came for Mary to have

the baby, and she gave birth to a son. Wrapping him in cloths, she put him in the manger.

The same night, the shepherds came to that lowly barnyard stable. They were looking for their newborn Savior. When they caught a glimpse of the baby Jesus resting peacefully in a manger, they couldn't stop rejoicing. "A multitude of angels told us about this newborn baby," the shepherds exclaimed to all who would listen.

Some time later, the wise men also found the baby. They too bowed to worship Jesus— the child they recognized as the newborn King. They laid expensive gifts of gold, frankincense, and myrrh at his feet. Afterwards, they went their own way, for they had been warned by God not to return to King Herod.

Even Simeon and Anna were able to see the baby Jesus. They knew that Jesus was someone special; he would fulfill all of God's promises. Israelites—from Abraham to King David—had looked forward to Jesus' arrival. Now, Simeon and Anna could see him with their own eyes! This little baby in their arms was not only a

descendant of King David but also God's only
Son, their Lord and Savior. He had come
to save all who believe in him. He had come
to set them free.

Bible Promise

*The Roman emperor, Augustus, decreed that a
census should be taken throughout the Roman
Empire. (This was the first census taken when
Quirinius was governor of Syria.) All returned
to their own ancestral towns to register for this
census. And because Joseph was a descendant of
King David, he had to go to Bethlehem in Judea,
David's ancient home. He traveled there from the
village of Nazareth in Galilee. He took with him
Mary, his fiancée, who was now obviously
pregnant.*

*And while they were there, the time came for
her baby to be born. She gave birth to her first child,
a son. She wrapped him snugly in strips of cloth and
laid him in a manger, because there was no lodging
available for them.*

—Luke 2:1-7

Prayer

We praise you, O God. Today a baby has been born to us; he is your only Son, the Prince of Peace, the King of kings, our Wonderful Counselor, our Lord and Savior. Today with food and gifts, we celebrate his birthday; he is the greatest gift of all. Thank you for sending your Son to save us. Thank you too for the gift of eternal life. As the shepherds and wise men did years ago, we also bow to worship your Son and our Savior, Jesus Christ. Amen and Amen.

Family Activity

If you have an Advent wreath, light the Christ candle. Have a time of silent prayer. Thank God for sending Jesus. Then sing "O Come, All Ye Faithful."

> O come, all ye faithful, joyful and
> triumphant,
> O come ye, O come ye to Bethlehem;
> Come and behold Him, born the King
> of angels;

O come, let us adore Him, O come,
let us adore Him,
O come, let us adore Him, Christ the
Lord.

about the author

Jon Farrar is the author of *Praying God's Promises for Your Marriage* and is Acquisitions Director for nonfiction at Tyndale House Publishers. Jon has edited and contributed to a number of book and software projects, including *The Nelson Study Bible* and *LessonMaker*. He enjoys Christmas every year in West Chicago with his wife and son.

Other Nativity books from Tyndale

The Nativity Story—A novelization of the major motion picture. Best-selling author Angela Hunt presents a heartwarming adaptation of *The Nativity Story*. Hunt brings the story of Christ's birth to life with remarkable attention to detail and a painstaking commitment to historical accuracy.

Also available in Spanish.

Other Nativity books
from Tyndale

Why the Nativity?—Why Bethlehem? Why Jesus?
Why did God send his only Son to earth as a baby?
In response to *The Nativity Story* movie release,
David Jeremiah, in his hallmark style, explains for
believers and skeptics alike why it is important to
examine again the birth of Jesus.

Also available in Spanish.

Other Nativity books
from Tyndale

A Classic Nativity Devotional—
The Nativity is one of the most vibrant
traditions we celebrate today. This
Christmas, experience the wonder
and awe of the season through the
poetry and prose of such classic authors
as Martin Luther, Charles Spurgeon,
John Milton, Christina Rossetti,
Henry Wadsworth Longfellow, and many others.

Looking Forward to the Nativity—
Twenty-five daily devotions bring the true
meaning of Christmas home this season.
Written with families in mind, each
devotion is accompanied by a family-
friendly activity designed to help your
children understand how the baby Jesus fulfilled everything
God had promised from the beginning.

Available now in stores
and online!